On Reading Patrick Connors' Poet

Linda M. Stitt, *"Patrick Connors has been a mainstay of Toronto's poetry ~~~ for many of its burgeoning years. His work is immediately accessible, touching on familiar places in the mortal psyche, eliciting responses that reveal us to ourselves. He experiences life below the surface, encouraging us to recognize and appreciate the richness and wonder of the everyday and the familiar longings of the human heart."*

George Elliott Clarke, *"Pat Connors is an unpretentious and unassuming a poet as is his hero, that bard of the everyman and everywoman, Al Purdy."*

Bruce Meyer, *"Here is a voice whose precision, sense of focus, grace, and economy of language, are brought together in poems that are memorable and gifted. The beauty of these pieces is that if you blink, you will miss them. Keep your eyes open, and watch as Connors runs through his memories and his vision of what life can be."*

bill bissett, *"Patrick Connors talks ordinaree language with the thrill uv urgensee n vois 2 th world with all th implikaysyuns uv metaphysiks n mindful soul 4 renewal n change his work is sew thotful fashyund 4 xpressyun n art a wonderful reed"*

Dr. Georgia Wider, *"...a collection of accessible meditations on hockey and hotdogs and friends and faith. His work is local, tactile, and specific in imagery...Connors speaks in the language of a working-class hero, a true people's poet."*

Robert Priest, *"Patrick Connors deceptively plain spoken poems give us a man in need of unadorned truth...he lays bare the heart and hopes of a seeker whose urge to reach the true light of faith refuses to be distracted by baubles and trinkets. It is refreshing to read these poems of spirit."*

Max Layton, *"Strong, forthright expression of abiding faith."*

Lillian Allan, *"Here's a writer who spends much creative-time facilitating opportunities for other writers, so it's indeed a happy occasion to see his first collection take shape."*

John B. Lee, *"...the writer is attentive to the betterment of the self, and through the example thereby becoming an inspiration to others through what the written word aspires to achieve. Poetry becomes a beacon to follow driving inward and illuminating interior darkness, the lifting that cup of light to lips for the speaking and to the ear for the hearing."*

Stanley Fefferman, *"...Connors courageously puts on paper what's in his heart about himself and what he cares about: poetry., hockey, religion, family, politics and love. His plainspeaking is supported by a craftsman's attention to detail."*

The Other Life

The Other Life

Patrick Connors

With Introduction By
Terry Barker

Library and Archives Canada Cataloguing in Publication

Title: The other life / Patrick Connors ; with introduction by Terry Barker.

Names: Connors, Patrick, 1969- author.

Description: Poems.

Identifiers: Canadiana (print) 2020037771X
Canadiana (ebook) 20200377809

ISBN 9781771615402 (softcover) ISBN 9781771615419 (PDF)
ISBN 9781771615426 (EPUB) ISBN 9781771615433 (Kindle)

Classification: LCC PS8605.O566 O84 2020
DDC C811/.6—dc23

Published by Mosaic Press, Oakville, Ontario, Canada, 2020.

MOSAIC PRESS, Publishers
www.Mosaic-Press.com
Copyright © Patrick Connors 2020

Printed and bound in Canada.

Designed by Rahim Piracha

MOSAIC PRESS
1252 Speers Road, Units 1 & 2, Oakville, Ontario, L6L 5N9
(905) 825-2130 • info@mosaic-press.com • www.mosaic-press.com

For my Love

Acknowledgements

Terry Barker has been indispensable to me, as he has been to so many poets and people, especially in forcing me to make this manuscript better. He also regularly helps me solve the problems of the world, usually on Tuesday nights.

My poetry really grew by working with Mick Burrs. He showed me how to make a poem much better by changing only one word, that there is always the potential to make a poem a little closer to perfection, and to love and cherish the process.

Luciano Iacobelli published my first two chapbooks, and gave me written permission to reprint these poems. His collaboration and friendship have always been highly valued and greatly appreciated.

Richard (tai) Grove has also previously published my work, and given me written permission to reprint. Thanks to him, and the CCLA, I had the opportunity to spend most of a week in the beautiful pearl of Gibara, Cuba, an experience I will always treasure.

James Deahl has always believed in me, supported me, and provided me with or connected me to opportunities only a more established writer could expect. I will always be grateful for his hospitality and mentorship.

For well over 40 years, I have been a charter member of the Torrance Road Hockey Association, although we don't play much anymore. These guys are like brothers to me; especially, of course, my brother Paul. The depth of relationship and experience we share is infused in many of these poems. I hope they will read my work, and get the "inside" parts.

Since it began in 2011, I have been involved in the 100,000 Poets for Change movement. In particular, I want to thank Dane Swan, Steve O'Brien, O. Puck, charles c. smith, Anna Yin, Brenda Clews, Georgia Wilder, and

Jeannine Pitas. We also collaborate on other projects, you have provided so many opportunities for me, and what we do together is a big part of who I am. I wouldn't have been able to accomplish any of this without my Mom. She is the best mother ever.

And, finally, to Inspiration. May it flow and continue to grow, may everyone be touched by this phenomenon, and may even one person be inspired by the words I have written.

Patrick Connors,
November, 2020
Toronto

Table of Contents

Introduction

Terry Barker

This first full collection of poetry by contemporary Toronto "People's Poet", M.C., and event organizer Pat Connors, carries on the tradition established in Canada's largest city by such local luminaries as Raymond Souster, and unsung home-grown heroes such as "the Cabbagetown Kid", Ted Plantos, and influenced by such national "people's poetic" paragons as Joe Wallace (1890-1975), Milton Acorn, and Al Purdy. Something of the (variant) spirit of all these founders of the form is present in Connors' contribution, well-displayed in this introductory volume, which contains many of the best-known pieces from his many readings.

Connors was born in Halifax, Nova Scotia, into a family from Newfoundland, but grew up in Scarborough, Ontario, the sprawling, largely working-class, eastern suburb of Toronto. Educated in local Roman Catholic schools, and at Toronto's downtown Ryerson University, where he studied English Literature and American History, Connors was influenced by Vatican II-inspired Roman Catholic social teaching, and the "leftist" thought he encountered in Toronto café society. However, while active in the "social justice" and somewhat arty literary circles of the central city, Connors did not cut his connections with East-end Toronto, or the Canadian East Coast.

Throughout this representative collection of Connors' work, eclectic in both form and subject, there is a persistent, indeed, plodding, expression of the unsatisfactoriness of our common temporal life, held together with hope for its improvement, and faith in the reality of a truth that is transcendent. This complexity of perspective, evident throughout the book, comes to a focus in the self-analytical poem "Madness", in which the poet finds relief from the insanities of contemporary life, extensively documented in the collection as a whole, in "the other life I live."

Connors'"other life" is, of course, the poetic, or, perhaps more accurately, that of the "poetry activist", for his life in and around "the poetry scene" (as opposed to the business world, where he makes his living), is clearly a conduit to the real life, which for him is spiritual, an expansion on the theme of his previously-published second chap-book, Part-Time Contemplative (Toronto: LyricalMyrical Press, 2016). In addition to the reading, writing and listening to poetry, and gathering together with fellow poets, Connors' "passage to the permanent" (as we might describe his "other life" in its full amplitude) is incarnated in the poet's enjoyment of team sports, the experience of Romantic love, the fellowship of "drinking buddies", the warmth of friendship and family, and the comradeship of political discussion and activism, as well as the security of membership in an historical faith community, themes which are all developed in this more extensive body of Connors' work, taken as a whole.

Ethical, rather than ethereal, in aim, the spiritual "message" of Connors' poetry is of the need for a critical Common Sense perspective in human affairs, and an affirmation of its potential presence, a fundamentally Aristotelian view of transcendence (in formal philosophical terms). This is an attitude detectable in the work of the prominent members of the Canadian People's Poetry tradition: Joe Wallace (like Connors), combining elements of Roman Catholicism and Communism; Milton Acorn uniting aspects of Marxism and High Anglicanism; Raymond Souster articulating the Social Gospel of his lifelong United Church fellowship; Ted Plantos exploring the "Christian Gnosticism" of the Romantics and esotericists; and Al Purdy, representing the contemporary contraction of reality into the contents of the Self, expressing definitively the Existentialist scepticism of all metaphysics, (whether traditionally religious or philosophical, or ideological), that has come to dominate the opinion-forming classes of Atlantic civilization.

Marmora, Ontario People's Poet Chris Faiers, winner of the inaugural Milton Acorn People's Poet Award (1987), has written that Pat Connors' "poetry reminds me of two other poetic recorders of (Toronto), Ted Plantos and Raymond Souster", all three are poets of place". Faiers finds that "there are especially similarities between (Connors') poetry and that of Ray Souster." Faiers fleshes out this perceived parallel as follows: "Ray's turf was the west end (of Toronto), and Patrick's poetry further adds to the canon of Toronto poetry, filling in the northeast quadrant, the (former) borough of Scarborough...

In addition to poetically documenting Toronto, both love sports, especially baseball, and both Patrick and Ray write about their deeply held Christian faith, but neither is dogmatic...Ray passed several years ago. In this (book), (The Other Life)...you will meet (his) successor, the next generation of Toronto's people's poets, Patrick Connors."

While drawing inspiration from many sources, Raymond Souster stated that his chief poetic models were the "three (American) Kenneths", the mid-Western urban "Populist Poets", Kenneth Fearing, Kenneth Patchen, and (less significantly) Kenneth Rexroth. Where Souster applies the down-to-earth, and yet gently transcendent, consciousness he found in these American poets to the circumstances he knew so well in "the Junction", "Swansea" and "Baby Point", and other areas of Central and West Toronto, Connors writes with a parallel, although more caustic, ironic and hortatory perspective (to that of Souster), of the Scarborough, "Beaches", "Danforth" and other East End or Central Toronto scenes of his life experience.

Connors, born in 1969, has some familiarity with American history and poetry, but if putative U.S. progenitors for his poetic perspective are to be sought, these might be located among the heirs of the Transcendental-ists, whose "human potential" viewpoint dominated the American "New Left" Movement of the 1960's. For Roman Catholic Americans caught up in the "changing times" of Vatican II and the "youth revolution", a Roman Catholic Transcendentalist journalist, essayist, political historian, activ-ist, and poet, Orestes Brownson (1803-1876), attracted renewed inter-est. Noted for his experience in the incipient trade union movement, his interest in sociology and the Spiritualist/Intuitionist moral philosophy of Frenchman Victor Cousin, and his pellucid prose and accessible poetry, the largely self-taught Brownson became an obvious starting point for Roman Catholic social thinkers of the U.S. "Sixties Generation", scholarship of the period noticing the important influence of Brownson upon the development of American socialism, and particularly Marxism.

Brownson's work is a suitable starting point, also, together with a reading of the late Gregory Baum's Catholics and Canadian Socialism, for a full apprecia-tion of "the other life" celebrated by Connors in this ground-breaking collection.

September 2020

Exit Poll
Advice to the New Leader

1. Promises are made to be broken,
   --like rotten eggs--
   but not until the morning
   after the election.

2. The current state of affairs
   is merely your reaction
   to mistakes *others* made in the past.

3. Give the people what they want
   --visions of fresh young faces,
   sunny summer picnics, and
   reduced deficit spending--
   but don't let them realize
   a better tomorrow.

4. Because the next administration
   will have to
   take it
   back!

5. Fiscal restraint is what makes
   our civilization *great*--
   or, at least, it will keep
   the current system
   chugging along a bit longer.

6. A balanced budget
          should *almost* make up
                for all those pesky poor people.

Hangover

The morning after the election
which changed the whole world
the sun rose faintly.
I got out of bed
pulled the cord to open the blinds.

I slowly made my way to the washroom
checked my dry tongue in the mirror
wobbled my way toward the kitchen
stopped to pick up the paper.
Ignoring the news, I opened the sports page.

Read about the Leafs latest loss – boy did they lose
put together the contents of my lunch
laid out my clothes – better wear a sweater
had peameal bacon and pancakes
for breakfast – just like every Wednesday.

To the Point

The best poems are written to be read by anyone.
Meticulously crafted over a period of time
To seem written
                    quickly and simply.

The best moments in life
are the result of years of preparation
passing by in a burst
causing change
                    even if you are not ready.

Before you realize
they have happened
                    they have happened

and stay with you forever.

The Rooster and the Piglet

Mid-day in January I sit alone
at La Perla Hermosa in sweltering heat
organizing my thoughts so I can record them.

Close by, the rooster and the piglet
perform the one-hundred-and-eighth rendition
of their one-hundred-and-eight act dialogue.

The rooster crows around the clock
as if it were always the break of day
waits one or two seconds for the piglet's reply—

if the piglet doesn't reply, the rooster crows again.
Sometimes, the piglet bleats, and the rooster waits
three or four seconds before he crows again.

Sometimes, they cry at the same time.
Sometimes, a yelping dog will join them.
In spite of this, I slept well last night.

I have done nothing since I got here
except share two meals with friends old and new.
I don't know when my next meal is, or how to ask for it—

but I am relaxed.
I know in a few days I must return
to my ordered and organized life—

I don't want to, yet I will also be happy when I go back.

Freedom

We are in a place where only now matters.
The art and science of planning
are thrown into the warm salty ocean
pulled away from shore by the undertow.

No agendas, no ulterior motives, only genuineness.
Share and experience yourself, each other—
a meal you would never have eaten before
that could be the best one of your life—

with a couple of beers to quench
the thirst you can only get
in a place like this—but I
do not need more than enough.

A people I love but don't always encounter
embrace me as one of their own
like we have known each other
longer than I have been alive.

My gracious host says, "It is a good thing
you are here, amigo, in the real Cuba
while it still lives, now that the embargo
has been lifted, before the changes come."

I want to support them, whatever this means.
I want to be a part of this place, their lives.
Forever I will carry this desire
in my heart as a part of me.

The Children

Don't blame the children.
The way of the world is not their fault—
it is my generation that has caused this mess.

We used to believe
in things like ban the bomb and free the whales
until we grew up and got jobs, and accumulated things.

Love the children.
Even though they are so big and loud and youthful
they are also beautiful and fragile, and they need our help.

It's time to believe again.
It's time to get beyond fear and comfort.
It's time to feel something else before it's too late.

Listen to the children.
They are the future, and they know
how to change and make everything better.

Remember we *all* once had this glorious hope.

An Open Letter to the Prime Minister

First of all, I want to give you
My sincere congratulations;
Only a brilliant opportunist
Could turn a vote of non-confidence
Into an overwhelming success

You see, I have voted PC
Not just because they are
My initials

Probably in some vain attempt
To make a misplaced
Appeal to paternalism

I am an ordinary average guy
I know Joe Walsh songs, listen to Rush
I love hamburgers and French fries
But tend to lay off the gravy – MSG
Sends my body messages
It doesn't seem to understand

I love to watch the game with my boys;
Few conversations begin without,
"How about them Leafs, or Jays, or
Raptors, or…"

I am a small-l liberal
Who has hugged
            far more trees than women
Although I much prefer the latter

You say everyday people
            don't care about art
Surely, *you* are not a
            cultural elitist

Furthermore, as a self-professed
            Evangelical Christian
I'm sure you believe in giving glory
            To God in any way possible

And that even such common vessels
            Should have every ability and
Occasion to do so
Stephen Harper is to muse
            As his politics are to amuse
The non-voting public

As long as we don't take a stand
            We the people have a hand
In conservative rhetoric

Since we're stuck with each other
            For five more fulfilling years
I have confidence that you and I
            Mr. Prime Minister and the typical guy

Can come to some sort of compromise:
            I will go on reading poetry
While you can go on telling lies

All the Way Down There
Inspired by No Other Country

It was in the province of Newfoundland
the land of my forefathers and one mother
where Al Purdy went to do the deed.

Incidentally, do not call it new-found-land.
Although this is how it is spelled, the word is not
pronounced that way by those who know better.

Nor is it to be called new-fn-lund—
the attempt to rhyme the last two syllables
always seemed bizarre to me.

Perhaps it is meant as a partial concession
between mainland sensibility and local dialect.
Just call it New-fn-land, if you please.

Al Purdy wrote an essay about Harbour Deep
the sort of rugged, frontier village
on which our nation was built.

Al Purdy tells us of a place with no roads
no police or doctors, where nearly everybody lives
on summer salmon fishing and autumn unemployment.

Al Purdy tells us about people named Loders, Cassells
Pollards, and Randells, with whom he had much in common—
only instead of cutting mattresses, they cut fish bellies.

Al Purdy was a gypsy—
he lived and felt more of Canada
than most of us have seen on TV or in a book.

By writing about these places and
the people who made them more than
a dot on a map, he tells us about ourselves.

Order
With a Shoutout or Two to Rudyard Kipling

I'm not here to change the world order
nor interested in revolution, just evolution:
where we all grow and work together
to help bring order to the world.

If anyone doesn't have enough to eat,
anywhere in a world full of plenty.
If anyone cannot be all they desire to be,
to grow and become the divine design.

If anyone does not have access to health care,
essential service as a basic human right.
If anyone does not live in security,
the dignity and respect of their humanness.

Even I, as a White, Anglo, Hetero,
fully able, highly educated, 1st world Christian
cannot understand why we won't accept difference,
and embrace the beauty we all have in common.

If you are ready to believe it's time for anyone who
realises these conditions to realise these conditions,
from the ones you love the very most
to the one you think your worst enemy.

If you are ready to believe it's time to change
things for the better before they get worse—

Then yours is the world and everything in it
           my sisters and brothers.
All the hopes and dreams and pains and sorrows
           and sufferings and joys:

You are now part of it.
Especially, if you weren't before.

When My Worlds Collide

My world was always meant to come together.
To have flow, unity, and coherence.

Even as a little boy, I lived in many worlds.
Problems always would arise when they would collide.
Especially when I forced them to.

Now, I live in that flow, embrace my reality,
        the uniqueness of who I am.
I accept the differences of all the worlds in which I walk.
I love each one of them individually, as well as part of
                a collective blessing.

Now, when my worlds collide, there is no confusion,
                        no fear, no resentment.
And I am free to be myself, not the guy I am
        within any crowd.

Now, I can try to help make the world
        the kind of place I have always wanted to live in.

Now that my life has begun.

The Beginning of Forever

I open my mind and start to see
my brothers and sisters, not obstacles—
buses are never late, rain does not fall
just to piss me off or make me sour.

Inheriting inherent possibility
every trial has the stuff of greatness.
When ready to endure all for the truth
I humbly pursue absolute hope and joy.

Trusting in the power behind it all
when I cannot make sense of it for myself.
I let go of all preconceived notions
and feel an occasional surge of faith.

Secure in the proof of what I live for
won't tear up like a bard, I am solid.
Though eager to get where I want to go
I willingly await eternity.

Never so excited for what might be next—
promise fulfilled when I let myself
let myself be loved as I love
and even more than I dared to dream.

Unity forged in refining fire,
anointing oil, sacred water cleansing—
indelible mark, undeniable sign
blessed beyond what I ever believed.

A Rhetorical Question
for
William Carlos Williams

How can I say
in one minimalist
yet run on sentence

separated into
a dozen or so lines
with little punctuation

something meaningful
something memorable
as I try to do

in my standard
long sweated over
six stanza poem?

The Professor
for Neil Peart

Floating on a grey-dark quiet-loud
wet-warm comfortable cloud
for, they say, the last time.

Tears run down my face
in total atonal harmony –
I did not plan it this way.

Staccato dreams of La Villa Strangiato,
Geddy's definitive sound, Alex's solos,
the beat of our collective heart.

You have turned the tip-tips and taps
and thump-thumps and ba-pa-dumps
of disenfranchised nerdy young men

into something resembling music—
the most meaningful music
I have ever known.

Begin the day with the friendly voice
to mould the new reality—
his love and life are deep.

For those who think and feel
good work is the key to good fortune
a thousand years have come and gone.

And the meek shall inherit the Earth.
And the meek shall inherit the Earth.

As it stands me and you may not collaborate
on the words which define two generations
transcending all religion

eliminating the need for politics
the exchange of currency other than
ideas and true love.

But thank you, just the same.

The Innocence of Youth

Erasmo's Nutella sandwiches
were bigger than Journey
back in Grade 6

to the point where he
only rarely got to eat them.

One day I decided it was my turn -
I was sick of hearing about
but not trying this great delicacy -

I was tired of feeling left out
and even more of peanut butter.

Erasmo tried to stop me
put up more resistance than usual
but I wasn't taking no for an answer;

I was amazed by the smooth texture
interrupted by chunks of chocolate I never had before.

For the next hour I felt elation
having tried this great taste treat
savouring even more a sense that I belonged

until I found out through the grapevine
Erasmo's Mom had put Ex-Lax in the sandwich.

The Bluebottle Fly Trapped in the Blue Bottle

Bluebottle fly trapped in a blue bottle—
        it had gone off course
disoriented by the heat of a summer night
the odour of a mosquito repellent torch
        or the loud music
                of a backyard party.

A boy up past his bedtime
picks up the bottle to show
the bluebottle fly to his sister.

She cringes but doesn't look away—
not the reaction he wanted.

He reaches back to throw the bottle—
ignoring his imploring sister—
guaranteeing he will do it.

The bottle twirls through the heat
of the night air, through the smoke
of the torch, vibrated by every pounding note
of the loud music
              at the backyard party—

further disorienting the bluebottle fly
trapped in the flying blue bottle.

Arencibia's First Homerun
I Remember Where I Was

Saturday afternoon at the ballpark
Hungering for a Spadina hot dog
With sauerkraut and honey mustard
Forgetting, for some reason
        why I can't get one

Move over to the open concession
I stand next to my two cousins
Trying to be the other brother
A part of the conversation
        or at least not apart from it

When, suddenly, Arencibia hits
His first home run, on his first pitch seen

35

My brother has turned on a milestone
nearly as bald and old as I am.

While I remember hearing him say,
"Don't trust anybody over 35!"—

I know he yet still has
364 more days
to become unreliable.

Train

Morning rush hour –
crowds of expressionless people
hurry to get somewhere
they would rather not be.

Human pinball on the platform
crashing hard against
the shoulders of a big man
try to carom lightly off a smaller one.

In my hot-tempered days
I would have embraced the conflict
but now all I can think about
is trying not to hurt my knees.

A New Approach

Some of us make the questionable claim
Which supports kicking ass and taking names
If it's against the code, I'll take the blame
But I will kiss hands while I do the same

Years and years I wasted, hopelessly spent
Portraying something I'm not, could never truly
Create a caricature for those who came and went
Showing signs of sides of myself superficially

A lifetime it seems I've wistfully yearned
For a perfect love which confirms and makes me
Everything I want, am supposed to have by now
But I always go back to being one of the guys

Then came the moment when time stood still
All the stars in alignment; my song comes on
Magic and chemistry and bravery alight the fire
As I fell upon the way I am finally ready for

I've gotten drunk, fought, played hockey, quite often
At the same time - made sport and mockery of my fate:
If I am to become the man I am to become
I have to stop being the one others would have me be

Hoops

Soot was the Harrison family dog
Everyone in the neighbourhood felt
    Like she was theirs

The Harrison family trained her
    To jump through hoops, sit pretty
Put up with a number of very young kids
    And be utterly adorable

I last saw Soot's picture
    When Cyndie was taken from us
God rest their souls –
    I cried that day for them both

Many days since have been a struggle;
    I don't dream of the times of chasing Soot around
But rather to pursue the dreams
    Which have beckoned me for almost as long

How many more hoops must I jump through
    How much more must I endure
Before I can live my truth

A Guy Like Me

"I wanted to write a poem
that you would understand.
For what good is it to me
if you can't understand it?"
William Carlos Williams, from "January Morning"

An autumn morning, Thanksgiving weekend, 1990
Mr. Harrison unlocked the front door
of his Haliburton cottage.

He was greeted by yours truly
tousled mullet above my ashen face
stammering and slurring good morning.

I hopelessly wanted to hide the evidence
of empty bottles and full ashtrays.
At least I had put the dope away.

In the next room, his youngest son
and three of our fellows
struggled to rouse themselves.

Mr. Harrison for the day exchanged
his mechanics coveralls for swim trunks
so we could help him *heave* the dock in for the season.

29

After a moment which seemed an hour
he broke the awkward silence asking,
"Pat, you are a writer, right?"

"Yessir", I replied, although I spoke
far more in those days about being
a writer than actually writing.

"Have you heard of Al Purdy?"
"Yessir, I have." Mr. Harrison smiled,
"I always thought you would write like him.

"He writes in a way
that a guy like me
could understand."

Bud's

Already trapped inside
          As more snow pounds
                    The cellar window
False sense of security
          from
                   being dumped on
          yet being warm

Three men related because
                 they married three sisters
Completely in lack of
          a sense of comfort
     of commonality
              Beyond the standard conversation,
                The eternal frustration;
                  the local pro hockey team

Realizing they have no place to go
                So
             they had better get along

"What we need," the oldest one ventures, rubbing his beer-bloated abdomen, "is a power forward with some upside."

"What we need," the next one interjects, as he favours his balding pate, "is a number one defenseman not on the downside."

The other one isn't sure what to say.
    He's not a hockey guy.
        He's had too much to drink.
            The youngest one in the group.

But he is smart, and wears thick glasses: He decides to state the merely obvious.

"What we need," with a sense of surprise and shock, "is a goalie who can make a save in the shootout."

They grunt and groan, guzzle their drinks,
            Belch and break wind,
    Rub bare toes in shag carpet
          Knowing they are all right.

Burby

Strange rectangular formations
stain the walls of schools
in Toronto's inner city.

Many rectangles are made of chalk
and are largely washed away
by each passing rain.

Some rectangles are painted or taped on
retaining the basic shape
they have held for over 30 years.

An outsider might think this to be
the result of a street gang marking territory
or proof of a superior life form
making their presence known.

To those of us who grew up
in Toronto during the 70's and 80's
they are the record of a pastime
invented here called *Burby*.

Seven innings, two outs
three players per side
flailed away at a tennis ball
with well-worn bats.

We aimed for home runs—
there were no placement hits.

On Summer days too hot for baseball
or mowing the lawn or digging post holes
we sweated and burned in the sun
to gain a small victory or live out a dream.

Then, we would smoke, mix up the teams
find somewhere indiscriminate to urinate
swig lukewarm orange pop from glass bottles
smoke again, and play seven more innings.

What Runs Through

We went to the Blue Jays game one Saturday
to see that damn Yankee Derek Jeter one last time.

Actually, it was also the first time
we saw him play in person,
at least together.

We participated in a standing ovation for Jeter—
something I *never* thought would happen.

Best of all, or almost best of all,
Jose Bautista hit a home run, and
our Blue Jays were victorious!

In the days of our youth, rarely did a week pass by
without attending at least one game.

The two of us would meet at Eglinton GO Station,
and, after a short wait, quickly get away from
what we didn't want to talk about.

We would talk about Moseby, Barfield and Bell—
and Dave Stieb and Dr. Henkenstein—
and whether this would be the year
we would finally break through—

while we passed by the factories and vacant lots,
subdivisions and shopping malls of suburbia.

We would arrive at Exhibition Stadium,
already a monument,
more historical than functional.

We knew guys who worked there—
they said rats ran
around the bleachers
just before batting practice.

Where did the rats go during the game?
Was it safe to go to the washroom,
especially on a cold day?

After the game we would go back to Eglinton,
and, being underage, use creative means to acquire beer.

Shortly after dark, we would enter
the forest inside McCowan Road Park to drink.

Every time we dug a new fire pit
or post holes to support a log to sit on,
we always uncovered decades of garbage.

The forest, the park, and the public school
were all built on a dump.

Purple poles positioned throughout the park
allowed pungent methane gas to escape

preventing mini-earthquakes from happening—
at least *most* of the time.

The creek, basically sewage,
running through McCowan Road Park
originates in the Don River.

We drank the beer complaining that it cost
nearly twelve dollars for twelve bottles.

We talked about the game, who was pitching
the next day, and when we would go again.

Or, we might plan to go to the video arcade,
or to play burby, if circumstances allowed.

We would nurse our last beers,
even talk about things rarely talked about,

in an effort to stay out long enough,
for everyone at our homes to fall asleep.

Now, we don't go to games much anymore,
although we are as close as ever.

Maybe it's because we can't spend
as much time with each other.

Maybe it's because we no longer
innocently believe in baseball's ability
to take us away from our problems.

Maybe it's because we don't have
anything at home to run away from.

Teenager

Look out the wind-blown window
Through the evergreen tree gone bare
Sun unseen lights the grey sky
Of air so cold even time is slowed
Until a bitter, vengeful gust
Threatens to take down the tree
The snow-covered roof of the house -
All which is on the horizon;
Try to sink deeper under the covers
And feel secure in knowing this
Is the most peaceful moment of the day

In the House Where I Grew Up

The kitchen table
In the house where I grew up
Was wooden, cold and stained

Came apart in the middle
Like so many ruined meals
And other realities hard to digest

Silences which say more than words can say
Furtive glances the only I love you
Support incomplete, bond left unspoken

When we left the house where I grew up
The kitchen table stayed behind
But the dining room table came with us

A place to spend and fear the holidays
An anchor to hold us to our past
When we did not know how to be a family

My Father the Poet

When I was 13,
I was already a poet
but I didn't even know it.

You see, I was a 'hockey guy', and
hockey guys weren't into poetry and
Stevie Wonder and romantic comedies and
sharing their feelings and all that stuff.

My grade 8 teacher, Mr. Nazar
gave us an assignment to write a poem
on whatever we wanted it to be.

I went home and played a game of street hockey
watched a rerun of M*A*S*H
and listened to my Rush album.

Then, later that night, looking into
the dying embers in our fireplace
I decided to write a poem about loneliness.

I figured I was an expert, the only
13-year-old in the world who knew
anything about that subject.

(If only I had known how lonely
some of my classmates were.)

I wrote, and wrote, and wrote.
I really, really enjoyed it
felt even more myself than while
gliding on a sheet of ice.

I finished the poem
but wasn't done
so I wrote another one.

When I was finished
I cried tears of healing
of self-discovery and accomplishment –
I felt less alone.

I couldn't figure out
which poem to hand in
I liked them both so much
and so differently.

So I gave them to my Dad to decide.
After all, he was the one I looked up to
not as a hero, or role model, or mentor
mostly as a demagogue with veto powers.

After about twenty minutes, he cursed them both
denounced them as crap, worse than crap;
he made me burn them in the fireplace.

To this day, this haunts me
spiritual warfare and mental anguish
neatly packaged and labeled as
the myth called, "Writer's Block".

Why would he make me burn a poem?
Why was everything I did *crap*?
Why wouldn't he let me do my best
in school, hockey, and life?

The rest of my adolescence was marked
by my attempts to define and express myself
and my Dad thwarting me at every turn.

When I turned 39, I submitted two poems
in honour of my first headline reading
to a website celebrating my family's ancestry.

Venerable Jack, the keeper of the domain
said in reply, "Ah, young cousin from Upalong,
you are indeed a poet, just like your old Dad!"

At last, although I had never known
I finally understood.

I forgive my Dad for this and
so much more I might be able
to write about with clarity after
twenty more years of therapy.

Panic

Your heart pounds against your ribcage
hopelessly trying to break free.
Your brain and eyes ache from the pressure
of blank thoughts beyond focus.

Your hands shake restlessly.
Your stomach churns and turns
as if you had consumed
something sour or tainted.

Your muscles tense until cramped.
Your hands and temples bead with sweat.
The harder you try, the harder it is
to catch your panting breath—

as you run an internal race
you cannot imagine ending
while to all external appearances
you are merely sitting still.

Recovery

It took oh so long to get myself straight
Doubtfulness delaying all the right things
Herbal teas, mysticism, oral fixations
Wise words written by those from before me

Take lots of advice, some good, some not;
Whatever you do don't try to heal too fast
Except if you accept or grin and bear it
Growth and change are inevitable

Played the fool by truth that was yet not truth
No one will take pity on feeble attempts
Such contrived representations: unless you
Want them to, and you don't want them to

Picked myself up and dusted myself off
Chose to contradict - to deny my demise
Sang my song out loud without audience or reason
Smiled and laughed and revelled in it all

Ready to live for the here and what's next
Forsake the past, the need to make right by
Fulfilling adolescent fantasies
Made of cathartic Hollywood endings

I had to look within while I was doing without
We all need to find one another but
The key to my recovery lay in
The discovery of what makes me me

Ready

A poem is the sunrise after darkest night;
an unexpected answer to much fervent prayer.

It is grace extended from a neglected muse,
only asking to be shared and seen, heard and felt.

A poem is inspiration
quickly recorded before lost,

cut down, built up, cut down again,
until it's ready to be read.

Esperanza
after Ferlinghetti

I have been waiting my whole life to write this poem.

I am waiting to realize my dreams, or, rather, the opportunity to act on them.

I am waiting for a time when love is the purpose of the rule of law.

I am waiting for an era where long lineups, aggressive drivers, and people who won't move back on the bus are the biggest problems.

I am waiting for a world where all the –isms disappear, only to be replaced by tolerance, peace and harmony.

I am waiting for more tolerance, peace and harmony in my own life.

But I know the waiting is good, because it helps me focus and work on what I'm waiting for.

I am waiting to forgive all the people who have wronged me over the years, and myself for all the times I've done wrong.

I am waiting for the end of hangovers…and my reliance on what causes them.

I am waiting to understand the purpose of the chronic pain in my knees, my heart, and my soul.

I am waiting to become patient, and I don't know how much longer I can wait.

I am waiting for her who has waited for me even longer to make our love bloom.

I am waiting for the next coming of my Lord and Saviour, even though He is in my life every day.

I am waiting for other people who call themselves Christians to realize He is coming back to save *everyone*.

I am waiting for what makes my waiting worthwhile.

Credence

I believe in God, whom we may worship in any way fitting, as long as it is a dogma based on reverence; tolerance and respect for all; a spirit which yearns for compassion and peace.

I believe in the dream Dr. King conceived. And if, indeed, it is to come to pass, our nation, Canada, shall be where it happens.

I believe in art, in truth, and beauty. All to which I humbly aspire.

I believe we are as saints when we are in fellowship.

I believe in the intrinsic ultimate goodness of all creation. Even the things that really tempt and test us.

Because I believe these things make us better.

I believe that much of what we think is wrong, though most of what we know in our hearts is right.

I believe in the life that is and especially in the one to come.

Renaissance

Integrity turns to courageous hope
Vision of what is and ought to be
Only if and when we are ready to
Believe there is no fear in perfection

Audacious belief in what seems unlikely
Fierce like the fire which consumes me
Blazing the trail as I follow it
Though I would rather not, I'll go it alone

Sorrow will surely lead to temptation
Reason to artfully dwell and wallow
We cannot beholden to the bottom
For from there is nowhere to go but up

Allowing the bounty of limitless grace
Growing in love we grow with each other
Bonding together, made ever stronger
Instruments of the divine by way of the sublime

The race we run, not a sprint,
But for the distance, we breathlessly seek
And find in each other by want and need
Delight and share as we follow the path

Does my heart seem to be open again -
After ages alone drifting in dreams
Of a time when anything could matter -
Breaking the barriers holding it down?

Universe which defines and shapes me
I long to fill you with how I feel
Boundless energy towards your creation
As you make me a part of your all

Long have I waited to be completed
Grown and felt and prospered and made ready
Every different day I approach the same
Until the one which makes everything new

Centre

I centre myself
To get closer to the Divine
Jesus Christ and the Holy Spirit
Who live inside of me

I must practice this every day
In every moment, every encounter
So I may seek my destiny
Aspire to full maturity

Turn, Turn, Turn

Give up your crooked ways
and your evil thoughts.
Return to the LORD *our God.*
He will be merciful
and forgive your sins.
(Isaiah 55:7, CEV)

The Earth will turn on its axis
until it will no more—
      hands on a clock turn slowly
      as do the tides and seasons—
so must I turn to my Lord
every day and be made new—

to get what I need to get through it
and a clean slate to fill
with fresh and recycled sins—

for even my best days
are marred by my mistakes,
decisions blurred by various vanities.

I will live the life
to which I am called
to give what I've been given
not just take and keep for myself.

Yet I drink from the cup the world gives me,
deeply as with a thirst that can't be quenched.

He will not change my circumstances
until He changes me and until
I let Him change me.

All There Is Is Everything

Beautiful vision, born of barren Earth
Can't really sense how we don't understand
Until seasons in time when we're not blind
Won't see all You said all along is true

I await You, for in faith You will come
When I'm made ready, not before Your time
I empty myself to make room for You
Feel my heart soar as it follows The Way

Learned the fear in impure imperfect love
Of torment and bitterness all alone
Transformed by the fire which fell like a dove
Never to leave us to be on our own

Moved by the force that started it all
Led by mighty enrapturing Spirit
Refreshed I take up the journey anew
Wherever it leads I'm ready to follow

I now know what I thought what was was wrong
No matter the times I'm not on my own
Own to my weakness I'm made ever strong
For inside Your arms I am never alone

Ours is not to question the reason why
Yet always embrace all which we receive
Give thanks and give praise, to serve and to share
All we are given, without hesitation

Please grant us the blessing to be aware
Forever we shall hear Your sweet wondrous voice
Amidst turmoil and noise from all around
That we may be founded upon the right choice

Let Me Be Drenched

The Lord will complete
what his purpose is for me.
Lord, your gracious love is eternal;
do not abandon your personal work in me.
(PS 138:8, ISV)

The storms they said were coming are here.
They are only beginning, still building up
power and fury to sustain the tempest
through this season and beyond.

Let whatever may come fall.
Let me be drenched.
Let it be my anointing
as I am made ready.

Please let me be
a part of your purpose.
Let me be a blessing
that I may be blessed.

I cannot but hope
to change the world—
and yet I can try
everyday.

The time has come
to take a stand
to no longer
wait on the sidelines—

to define what I am
and what I will be
in the face of adversity
which will only make me whole.

It doesn't matter
whatever storms may rage—
if they knock me down
I will get back up.

It doesn't matter
if my (future) church wedding
is on a rainy spring Saturday
or in the springtime of my life

because I know
my love is real and manifested
and when the timing is made perfect
the bond will last forever.

The storms and those who would be
their agents do not define me.
What I have and will have
cannot be taken away.

Epic

My feet
     set squarely in
             the present.
My eyes
     firmly focused on
                the future.

The narrow way
     seems dangerous and hard
wrought with strife
     and lonely.

But when not absorbed in
     seeming circumstances
or caught up in
           wavering from
side   to   side
it merely becomes
         the surest and shortest distance
    between two points.

The past has passed
          and the present is
               but a fleeting gift—

I will hold out for

                                 the future

and trust in

                          what it brings.

Birth, Rebirth

I cannot live without
A spirit of hope for this day
To see and feel eternal things
Bud and begin to bloom and breathe

Waiting, much like praying
And writing poems by hand
Builds up muscle and strength
Substance and depth

Cramps and pains are inevitable
They may seem final to some
But delay is not denial
Of what is to come

Open Ending

Poetic ideas expressed unpoetically
Stuck in left-brain thinking
The ought-to's of day-to-day life
Preoccupied with where I think I should be

When all I want to do is
Reach out and embrace the world
Like a hippie hugging a tree
And not worry that I can't even grow
A bad mullet anymore

I want to be where I am and
Be here more fully as always myself
Ready to grow and follow the journey
To go wherever this will take me

Toronto the Good

How many decent, lovely women
Pretty as first spring flowers
Promising young men, innocent bystanders
Wayward young offenders making mistakes
They cannot erase, ever forsake
Will it have to take
How much more yet still
For the powers-that-be to admit
Houston we have big problems
And whom shall solve them

Toronto the Good, ideals endangered
Violence repeals such grand reputation
This land is our land
We stand for the entirety
In some unclearly defined synecdoche
War unrefined unites us in
Dark starless nights of tragedy
Stark days after of mourning
Gunmetal shovels pouring new earth plant
Broken seeds that can't grow

Lives fade like Autumn leaves
Bodies laid to eternal rest
Those left behind never know
But where do we go

From here in our grief
To belief in the feeling
Of forgiving and grace, the
Place of healing and wholeness
As we redress sin and
Let the good guys win

Baltimore

A man has been treated as vermin to be squashed, like an afterthought of an afterthought, without regard to his essential humanity.
All because of a long rapsheet, a system lacking proven checks and balances, and the colour of his skin.
Because of this repeated, systemic injustice, people are rising up.
You're damn right it's dangerous and scary in Baltimore.
It seems it has been for a little while.

White Guilt

Just because my great Grandfather sailed a ship
Doesn't make him great, though he
Fulfilled a purpose to complete the Empire
Made sure a few of us did better than some
Do you understand?

I love all of God's people - beautiful - sweet smart strong
Basketball players, guys I used to
Jam with down in the neighbourhood
Back in the days of white chocolate shadow

My great Grandfather watched his own die
Of scurvy, imperialism, lack of scholarships
MIT, U of T, Rye High; he did what he could
To get us across The Pond to the New World
And I Memorially thank him

So I say if you don't know me then you don't
Understand my life and death as I understand
Your life and death, but if you do understand
My life and death, then you understand white guilt

Such As This
for Charles Roach

My well-meaning heart
cannot contain the world
or even its petty desires.

What lies outside of me
is bigger than I am –
the pains and hopes and dreams
of everyone I see.

So much more
than I can comprehend
exists in the land
I see and think I know.

Because
when I show up
at a moment
such as this.

Someone could be hungry
someone may have died
someone may be impatient for change
        other than me.

Someone may not want to hear
the sob story
I have prepared
for a moment
         such as this.

People's Poet

Mr. Purdy spoke plainly. I'm not saying he was simple, but rather that he wrote simply. Clarity and integrity were not merely touchstone virtues, but really a way of life. He didn't know another way to be. He didn't try to impress anyone – he didn't have to. He just was Al Purdy.

But he could also write about a hockey game in a factual manner which journalists could not capture without missing a detail lacking in artifice but not in artistry the stream of consciousness would not stop flowing harkening to Hemingway while pre-dating and necessarily leading to spoken word poetry even though he wouldn't have had any way of knowing this, the debt owed to him.

Mr. Purdy was a People's Poet.
People's Poetry is timeless.

All I Want To Be

Disconnect--
   the distance between
   where I am
   and where I want to be.

Dissonance--
   thinking all I am is wrong
   the notes of my song in discord
   until I don't even try to sing.

If only I had the strength
to live my life
as if I were living the life
of my poems and dreams.

Then I would be alive.
I would be of the light
I want shining through me—
but not just for myself.

I could create, and work, and be.
I would struggle, O Lord yes, I would struggle
every day for the rest of my life
or until the world changes – whatever comes first!

Become

Become the fulfillment of your dream
endure the sacrifice which you need
for your dream to become pure.

Appreciate who you are, what you have
be ready to change and grow from there
learn what it takes to overcome your fear.

Sometimes it doesn't seem to happen at the speed
or in the way you would like, but make no mistake
it is becoming, all you could imagine and more.

Every one of us has a path to take
which leads us on a journey beyond the realm of goals—
become and keep becoming the best you can be.

Really, Truly, Actually

Really I just noticed
Merely the most beautiful
Woman I have ever
Seen, while I am sure
(Though I can't say where)
We certainly met before

Planning for forever
Though it seems much longer
As I wait to discover
All I want to uncover
To share with each other
As we seek for Another

Truly, back in all those
Days I was lost
In a daze it was
Because of her
I thought I could never
Be with her
I could not ever
Have gotten
Over her
Or even moved on
With somebody else

Actually, ever since
The earliest memory of
When I came to life
Became the boy
Inside the man
Even before then
I have loved her

Something Mature and Very Unnatural
Written on the border of Scarborough

If I had but two little wings
And were a little feathery bird,
> *To you I'd fly, my dear!*
But thoughts like these are idle things,
> *And I stay here.*

Samuel Taylor Coleridge
> *From*
Something Childish, but Very Natural

At night in my mind I can fly
> In the day as I dare to dream
>> Of all that will come true
Until my soul cries out, asks why,
>> I can't see you

Although not doomed, all hope is gone
> Till I give up my hopeless scheme;
>> To enact in my time
What is destined to come anon -
>> And keep my rhyme

The Sun does shine, the Moon may glow
      Even in rain my face will beam
            The world is all one's own
For when we live for what we know
            None are alone

Sleep stays not though a monarch bids:
      Me to wait and let Him redeem
          What's won before;
Vision revealed - opened eyelids
            See all I sought and more

Things I Would Do for Love

Believe in myself, and, indeed, something else—
alter the way I have seen the universe
only by how you shall do so for me.
Call it making love instead of the other
and not fall asleep for five minutes after.
Eat supper with your folks every Friday
without wondering too much where the boys are.
Avoid high drama outside of ourselves
leaving the rest to deal with their own sh--
quit being a whiny crybaby emotional suck
in case that's what you need to be.

Certain feeling sought after for some time
followed hopeless dreams which drifted away.
Greater love than I already have surely lies ahead—
I must be patient.

I've never been one, as such, for the chase
though it's easier to do than to wait
and harder to be brave when standing still
while the world spins around without my input.

Stop watching hockey on Saturday night
or paying some other tribute to maleness.
Give to each breath a life of its' own
sharing and savouring every heartbeat.

Surrender my deep dark childish fears
to willingly change all for the better.
Put my persona up to scorn and ridicule
set apart from everyone and everything.
Cast aside my ego with all ills of its' ilk
as I lay myself on the proving line—
where do I sign?

Things I Must Be True To

My mind, my reason, my ideas
My morals, my values, my ideals
My heart, my Love, my soul
My spirit, my vision, my dreams
My Mother, my brother, my sister

                                        The Father

              My limited understanding
Of the universal flow
                    and
My role in it

               Those aspects left
Of my long-haired
Coniferous tree-hugging
Hippie mantra
            and my Toronto Maple Leaf loving
                   ingrown Hockey-haired mullet

               My family
Genealogical, spiritual, ecumenical
Incidental, philosophical, animal
Commercial, longitudinal, municipal
My neighbourhood, my country, my world
               And all who are in it

My passions, my reasons, my causes
The issues that I take issue with
That which ensues from that which I issue

                                  I stand up for
    The cause and effect
                                  Of that which I stand for

                                                    Truth

Before I can do this
                        While I aspire to all that
    At the end of the day
                                      Myself

The End of Some Things

The Sun flickers
through charcoal clouds
until 4 o'clock.

After 4 o'clock
                    it tries to warm

the memory of Summer—
        the memory always better
                than the reality.

Orange, red-brown, light green
leaves me feeling warm
like a bonfire which covers

my neighbourhood
with smouldering ashes—

last remnants of what was
alive only days earlier

foresight of what will fall
while the Earth lays at rest.

There is beauty
        in the change
                of seasons.

PoeTrain Haiku

Country passes by
outside of the nation's train
quickly but slowly...

Celebration Square Mississauga

Poetry and music
on stage outside at twilight –
for a moment it is Summer.

Somewhere Down the Zen River

Current runs smoothly
all stands still for a moment—
the eternal now

Bleeding Blue and White

Early season's hope
becomes Autumn's discontent—
my captain falls down.

Flow

The heart is the source
of all life and love - let it
continue to flow.

Found

Poetry came in
search of me – I stopped hiding
and soon found myself.

What I Learnt in Salesman School

If it looks like a duck and walks like a duck
and eats like a duck and sits like a duck
it's probably a duck—
even if you call it a goose.

Madness
For Suds

Einstein defined insanity
as doing the same thing

over and over again, while
expecting different results.

Yet here I am in the same predicament
I hoped to avoid

before, during, and after
becoming an adult.

Answering the call, I cater
to a ravenous, raging creature—

a starving need that cannot be sated,
only made hungrier by more, more, more—

bloated by excess with no escape
under the guise of helping myself.

The only thing
which keeps me sane

is the other life I live
during a few treasured moments

and the dream that one day
it will be the only one.

Fallow

Sun shines low in the sky.
Cool, clear, crisp air waves
gently across a fertile world—
it is time to sleep.

I am cold
dark, closed over.
Restless, nothing
has come out of me for some time.

Once formable clay
has become a shell of myself.
I have let the world trick me
into believing this is my reality.

I have become the result
of constant bitterness
of engaging in battles
not worth fighting.

I choke back life, swallowing
my tongue and tears until they are gone.
My face set like stone, my footsteps wary
I barely make it through another day.

Oh dear one, break me open.
Let the cracks bring in
fresh air, water and light
while the seeds within me can still grow.

The Longest Night

It has been dark about an hour.
I stand at the bus stop
shortly after 5, feet
freezing in big city boots
fingers tingle in leather gloves
more suited for fall or spring.

Tomorrow is winter
the year essentially over.
I look back on how I passed
the time in unsatisfactory work
serving mammon which provides
the means to cure my pain.

I wonder how next year
will be different, what
I can do to make it better.
I feel helpless, numb,
empty, and wonder
when my bus will get here.

Reprise

Fluorescent lights
dim perceptions
smiles flash for a moment

clock-watchers
computers warm up
conversation cools

another day has begun
in the sort of place
hoped to be behind me

where truths are discovered
sought for so long:

To be self-contained
as a contemplative

yet ready to be
part of everything

to not give into
idiosyncracies and insecurities
especially my own…

to love the unlovely
and love the lovable all the more

to work with energy, assertiveness,
and give the world its due
with consistency and integrity.

I am grateful for how
life is entirely different
after 5 PM, before 9 AM

The conversations are unscripted;
all I want from you
is to know how you are feeling

how your day has been
to share a meal with you
and maybe my latest poem

I am also grateful because
after 9 AM, before 5 PM
I am still the same person.

As if to spite myself
I have finally learned

never to be afraid
to be who I am

how to be alone
but not lonely

to not make trials worse
than they really are

to be aware of where I am
instead of dreaming
where I feel I ought to be.

Steps

In the north
You see the results
Of every step you take

You can hear each one, too;
The crunch of ice and snow
Might be the only sound
Above your laboured breath

Someone who follows
A few minutes behind
Can tell whether you are alone

If you slide your feet,
walk with a limp
Are using skis or a sled

Unless fresh wind or snow
Have covered your tracks

Each step takes you closer
To a destination you know
By faith, for by sight
Your pathway seems endless

Window

I imagine
laying down on
the middle
of the ocean—

looking down
through clean clear ice
at the very bottom
of the world—

wondering what
mysteries lie
on the bitter
rocky floor.

Vernal Equinox

The first sun of spring rises—
earlier than it has for many moons
slowly but certainly.

At first it is but a faint glow
a silhouette around the buildings
to the very north of me.

In the time it takes
to get the news of the day
and free the sports page from it

the shimmer of hope has become
a glimmer of promise fulfilled—
a hint of orange, an image of the warmth to come.

In the time it takes
to make coffee and breakfast
the sky turns grey and bare.

I want to wait inside
for the risen sun's warmth
to come and envelop me.

But I know it is time to go
and do the day's bidding—
waiting is not a passive activity.

I go out into the frigid morning—
yesterday was winter
today is but the beginning of spring.

Springtime in Canada

April snow billows and blows
but goes nowhere, with drifts
just long enough to cause accidents
which change lives forever.

Blustery wet wind rattles rooftops
topples and tears down trees
older than the neighbourhood around them
and makes small dogs pensive.

Springtime in Canada means we watch
children play hockey on outdoor rinks,
millionaires play baseball in domed stadiums
and say, "I can't wait until it's really Spring!"

It is planting seeds in unreceptive soil
hoping to make life out of nothing –
cold, cracked hands the mark of your labours,
and you know that the trying is worthwhile.

Inspiration

It took a sprained knee—
swollen, stiff, and sore—
to force me to take
a Saturday off.

No backyard barbecues
or epic excursions to the bar.
No agitated trips to a stadium
to support one of my teams.

No poetry readings
no requirements, real or imagined
other than to be here, to heal
and prepare for whatever comes.

I sat as still as I could
held an icepack to my knee
felt the breeze waft through
the screen of the sunroom door

tried to clear my head
remember a time I didn't feel weak
took an anti-inflammatory pill
and wrote the first draft of this poem.

Scenes from a Summer Afternoon

The young river washes cool water
over the banks of the muddy shore.

Above the mud, firmly rooted verdant
grass climbs into a gentle slope.

At the top of this hill, a tree younger
than the river reaches toward the sky.

Over the tips of the branches of the tree
the sun beams down light and warmth.

On a blazing, bustling big city sidewalk
a woman guides a man in a wheelchair.

They pass another man pushing a stroller
inside which a brother and sister sleep.

Closer to the curb, a young boy extends the gift
of a handful of change to a woman and her dog.

Across the street, a girl with tears in her eyes
gently places her teddy bear at a memorial.

Loaded Questions

A heavy mist becomes light drips
falling slowly from the dreary sky
signalling the end of summer.

I stand in my workday bus stop shelter
hand held outside the doorway
feeling the cool rain.

I ponder my lot in life,
or at least where I am right now,
and try to figure out what comes next.

Will the Maple Leafs sign Willy Nylander?
Are we due for one last warm blast?
Is today the day I get the big sale?

Will Canada Post go on strike?
Does the new government care about us?
How can we not lose everything we have?

The bus arrives. A gaggle of passengers
get off with a grimace. The driver says hello,
but doesn't ask how I am doing.

The people left behind on the bus spend time
they would rather not spend talking to each other
asking about their children and plans for the weekend.

The bus crawls along the thoroughfare
through a sea of patiently frustrated traffic
between banks of cookie-cutter high-rise apartments.

We pass over the railway tracks, alongside a clearing
with a grove of trees changing color - orange, yellow, brown -
and I wonder if I have ever seen anything more beautiful.

Me With You

All day climbing the corporate ladder
Up all night treating the pain
Sleep in late on alternate Saturday's
Wondering why it is all in vain

The blanket seems longer than it really is
Without a second set of legs, another body
To pull it out of the covers, from under
The mattress, to soak it in hot-cold sweat

Filling myself with emptiness
The things men do to define themselves
To get set apart by acting the same
When all I need is to be me with you

With you it's always like a dream
The rest a nightmare I must wake up from
I will have the reality for which I yearn
Until then both ends of the candle will burn

Lavalife Girl

If I could just get past the front page of the site
Portrayal of she who bewilders and beguiles me
I could perfect and polish my personal profile –
End of love problems in sight

I wonder if she truly looks like that
Or maybe she is even more wonderful
Without virtual fantasy betraying reality

I wonder if she would settle for cheeseburgers on a date
Green salad and French fries keep it casual
Or would I fall hard and feel compelled
To go for the steak, salade verte and pommes frites

I wonder if she is the sort of lady
Who, because of what she sees and perceives
Would put her self aside to enable and
Help you achieve everything you believe

Perfection and beauty come from within
The tears we cry when we are alone
Not just for someone but for the one
Who will help complete us

I wonder if she makes everyone she meets feel
They are the most important person in the world
With honest concern and not a trace of vanity

Wonder struck with questions
                For which there are only one answer:

I am amazed by her, enraptured by the miracle she is
I need her in my home, I need her for
                Meaning, balance; to aspire to my best
                I need her in my bed, in my arms, in my life

The Moon

Many of us revere the moon
a dark celestial body
which reflects Earth's light
by varying degrees

based on our wary movements
about a brilliant blazing Sun
making its rounds around us
in what we selfishly call a day.

The moon seems so alone—
the glow around it
doesn't allow us to see the stars
especially from our smog-ridden city

I can stare at it for hours
sing soulful songs from long ago
write first lines of unfinished poems
about everything we're missing.

Valentine

Love will bring you ecstatic explosions
which build you up and bring understanding.
But this will make you realize
no matter what you have believed
the truest love is not a fairy tale
and won't be achieved without sacrifice.

If you don't think so, remember
Valentine himself was tortured
and beheaded because of love:
he made friends with King Claudius,
even gained his favour, but refused
to renounce what was most dear to him.

He gave his all for a love
which has been and is immortalized.
In the same way, we all must
be prepared to pass through some trials
and become worthy of *this* love,
made ready for the one *you* love.

Waiting

Waiting, waiting

For the existence I used to need and strive for
one of excitement, accomplishment, satisfaction
before I boringly sold out to corporate dreams,
hockey pools, and other, lesser adversaries.

Waiting for my dreams to come true.
Dreams to change the world for the better.
My book gets published, wins the Nobel Prize!
No more hunger in Myanmar, Ethiopia, or Toronto...

Waiting

Waiting

For the time when I can live down a past
I didn't create but allowed to happen.
Assisted into being because it was
harder to believe than not to.

Waiting an eternity for the love
I will always love as I always have.
Forever reborn within ourselves, our self
in each other's arms we reach out to the world.

Unattainable

It's not that she's way out of my league—
successful, popular, widely admired
empowered, wise, mature beyond her years—
though she certainly is.

It's not that she has many friends and well wishers—
would-be suitors would shell out three days pay
for dinner, a dance, and a dream to spend
eternity with her; though she certainly does.

This couldn't be the first song sung for her
sweet portrait or exquisite depiction
of her heart-shaped face and rare haunting eyes
which cannot begin to do her justice.

Am I in my ardour the only one who can truly see
past her considerable trappings to all I wish to ensnare.
With diligence I await what shall come to be
yet ready to curse or do worse to any who would dare to disagree.

I am just a humble poet living
my workaday life of dateless wonderment
with nothing to offer her but these words
where they come from and everything they stand for.

When I say unattainable, it's not
because I am afraid of feeling like this
for the first time, perhaps the last
dare I to rush my steps like a fool.

It's because I trust in who she is and who I am
and that we could discover together
something entirely unfeasible and unreasonable
to all who do not know how to believe.

Scarborough Bar

Gap-toothed guy comes up as if to gum me
Waves his hand backwards, does his best John Cena
"You can't see me!" - laughs uproariously
As at something he's never done before
Searches his audience for approval
Then goes on his way to picking winners

Remember the days when this place was named
After fine cognac rarely ever served
Slow dancing with a beauty queen
Fulfillment of my wildest dreams
Then wishing she wasn't too young for me
Now glad we are finally right for each other

Places I cannot go anymore
Strongholds in my mind or roles to fit in
Though I crave them all as a piece of myself
Addition by subtraction leads to new doors
I must keep open and hope you will enter
Lesser boundaries and better bounties to share

ambiguity

The great unknown
Is the basis of art
The level on which we share
While I hold something back;
Leaving you to want more

Deep feelings and
Profound thoughts
Expressed under
The influence
The considerable
Duress of
Meeting an
       entirely
Self-imposed
Deadline

To be great
Completed
Or, at least
     known
By the time
I turn fifty-two

I have been a writer
For many years;
I have passed
Many years
Without writing

Fondly finish off with this
Hoping to be remembered by
What's not entirely explained;
And let you fill in
The blanks for yourself

What you have meant
As I become,
I have grown -

And hope you
Have with me

In the depth
Of my fears
At the end
Of my tears
I am strong

The Wonder

The years which have led me
into middle age
unwittingly, unwillingly
have yet been kind.

I have lost 20 pounds
I have gained strength, patience.
My eyes may not work as well
but I see much more clearly.

What I used to hate I now love
what I used to love I now adore
what I cannot change I accept—
what I can't accept I try to change.

I am not what I will be
I am not what I once was—
and yet I appreciate everything
which has brought me here.

Publications

Patrick Connors first chapbook, *Scarborough Songs*, was published by Lyricalmyrical Press in 2013 and charted on the Toronto Poetry Map. *Part-time Contemplative*, his second chapbook was also published by Lyricalmyrical in 2016. *Bottom of the Wine Jar*, published by SandCrab Books in 2017 contains 18 poems by Patrick Connors. His poetry has also been published in *The Toronto Quarterly, Spadina Literary Review, Tamaracks*, an anthology of Canadian poets published in 2019 in Long Beach, CA.